Sixty-Five Lively Ideas for Successful Aging

Marjorie Bayes, Ph.D.
and Bonnie Messer, Ph.D.

Illustrated by Susan Bell

Table of Contents

ISBN 978-1-4782295-2-0

Introduction

You may be ready to make some positive changes in your life as you grow older. We hope this book will help. While much is written about the problems of aging, we refocus the spotlight from losses to new possibilities for enjoying and thriving in late life.

Our information comes from social scientists who study "successful aging," defined as "getting a maximum of satisfaction out of life." Success involves finding meaningful ways to cope with or avoid typical age-related problems, and to seek interesting new choices. Clearly, an important aspect of successful aging is active engagement with life at whatever level is possible.

As psychologists who ourselves are over 65, we have tried to suggest actions that will promote mental and emotional resilience with age. Underlying our suggestions are basic ideas from researchers such as sociologist Sarah Lawrence-Lightfoot and psychiatrist George Vaillant, who study successful aging. Dr. Vaillant has some ideas based on several long-term studies, one covering more than 70 years, of how human strengths develop over a lifetime. In his book *Aging Well* and other writings, he describes the coping styles associated with successful aging.

In her book *The Third Chapter: Passion, Risk, and Adventure in the 25 Years After 50*, Dr. Lawrence-Lightfoot reports on a series of in-depth interviews with older people. She advises us not to be preoccupied with losses, but to shift the focus of our energies and priorities, to find "ways of changing, adapting, exploring, mastering, and channeling … energies, skills and passions into new domains of learning." By refocusing, we can nurture "an eagerness to engage new perspectives, skills, and appetites." She points out that moving to any new stage in our life span involves both losses and liberation.

We have built upon the research to identify seven categories of activities, with specific suggestions any one of us might be able to accomplish. The categories are: *Changing, Connecting, Learning, Creating, Helping, Managing,*

··· Changing ···
··· Connecting ···
··· Learning ···
··· Creating ···
··· Helping ···
··· Managing ···
··· Playing ···

and *Playing*. These chapters offer new possibilities--the freedom to develop new pleasures and habits, while retaining and enhancing some of the old ones.

We hope that among our suggestions you will find interesting choices, chances for freedom and fun and connection in late life. In his book *A Time to Live: Seven Tasks of Creative Aging*, clergyman Robert Raines reflects, "At our age, free of absolute inhibitions, we often can say and do what we want. What are they going to do to us?"

Poet Mary Oliver asks

"Tell me, what is it you plan to do with your one wild and precious life?"

Chapter One
Changing

"The transitions in life's second half offer a special kind of opportunity to break with the social conditioning ... and to do something really new and different."
–William Bridges, *Transitions*

Changing provides us with the opportunity to explore ways of exercising our mental and physical muscles. We don't have to give up all our comfortable, safe old habits, but we do need to be open to exploring new possibilities, new ideas, new things, and new people. Ultimately, we are strengthening our ability to adapt. Flexibility, resilience, adaptability—these are qualities important for any time, but particularly for later life when things can happen over which we have little control. Try some of these suggestions, for practice.

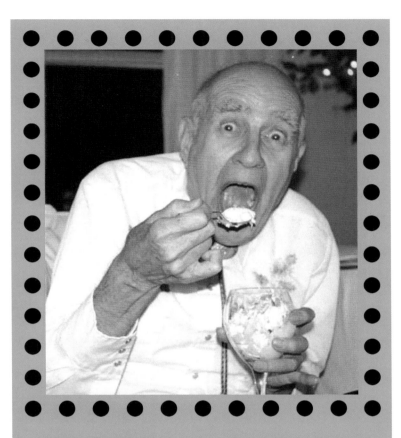

Try an unfamiliar food each week, preferably food
with odd names. Explore Middle Eastern, Indian,
Ethiopian, or Asian markets.

End a bad habit. Don't tell anyone.

For example, Buddhist teacher Pema Chodron says, "We could … lighten up and turn around our well-established habit of striking out and blaming."

Buy different brands of ordinary things, like toothpaste or shampoo.

Choose an unfamiliar spice (not salt or pepper) and use it daily for two weeks. Okay, one week. Try turmeric, rosemary, or paprika.

Wear or carry something unusual. Be prepared to share a story about it in case anyone asks why you have it.

Read a magazine in which you have absolutely no interest. Read it cover to cover, including the advertisements. Did you change your mind about anything? Why?

MSO EXCITING
AGAZINE

Special Issue
Watching Grass Grow

"Everyone has the power to make choices, but unhappy people don't know they have it … Choice is available to anyone who has the courage to exercise it."

–Dan Baker and Cameron Stauth, *What Happy People Know*

Climb Mt. Kilimanjaro–or the
equivalent in your own life.

Ann Fort, of Denver, Colorado, is active in mission programs and has made more than a dozen trips to Africa. She was always intrigued by 19,340 foot Mt. Kilimanjaro in Tanzania. In 2008, at the age of 84, Ann and a mission group attempted the six-day climb. After two days of climbing trails filled with rocks and boulders, at a little over halfway to the top, Ann chose to follow the directions on a sign which read,

"Don't go beyond this point."
Even though the message was in reference to not treading on the vegetation, Ann took it as a sign that she had achieved her goal: it was enough.

Learn a new game, like Mexican Train® or
Apples to Apples® or Sequence®.

Invite people of all ages to join you to play.

Take a walk at least three times a week, as you are able. Look for something new each time–the shape of clouds, the style of buildings, lawn or store window decorations.

Form an in-process group. Artist/writer Sark describes this as a group in which members help each other in reaching creative goals, sharing "questions, ideas, frustrations, and avoidances." That should also work for people whose lives are creative productions in progress.

Look for the parts of yourself you have neglected or given up sometime in the course of your life. Spend time in reflection; what would you like to do about it? Writer George Eliot said,

"It's never too late to be what you might have been."

Chapter Two

CONNECTING

*"In the end, when we look at our life,
the questions will be simple:
Did I live fully?
Did I love well?"*
–Jack Kornfield, *The Art of Forgiveness,
Lovingkindness, and Peace*

As we seek to age successfully, we can begin by building on our strengths. The capacity for empathy and compassion often improves with age. Seize opportunities to reach out and connect with others. Caring relationships remain critically important in later life, even influencing our physical health.

Listen. Give other people the gift of your attention. If you now have more time, use it wisely. Take a deep breath and really listen to others' dreams and joys and pains and questions.

Share your own stories. Be careful, however, that you do not repeatedly tell the same stories to the same people.

Stay in touch. Find old friends on Facebook®.
Send "Thinking of You" cards for no special reason.

Add a new friend to your life. Psychiatrist and researcher George Vaillant has found that one of the keys to contentment late in life is a growing circle of friends.

Challenge your stereotypes. It has been said that we fear what we do not understand. What do you fear? What could you do to increase your understanding? It's never too late to give up your prejudices.

Forgive someone. Dr. Vaillant's second key is "nurturing our ability to forgive slights and injuries … optimistic grateful forgiving." Buddhist nun Pema Chodron discusses the power in "letting go." You can choose to hold on or let go of jealousy, resentment, anger, stress. "You don't have to let go of the big things you're holding on to, because usually you can't … But even with small things … letting go can bring a sense of enormous relief, relaxation, and connection with … the genuine heart." Practice "letting go." Buddhist teacher Jack Kornfield says, "Forgiveness means giving up all hope of a better past."

While you're at it, ask for forgiveness from those you may have hurt or wronged. Author Maya Angelou says, "I've learned that people will forget what you said, people will forget what you did, but people will never forget how you made them feel."

*Go to hear local musicians
such as the Queen City Jazz Band.
Buy their CDs.*

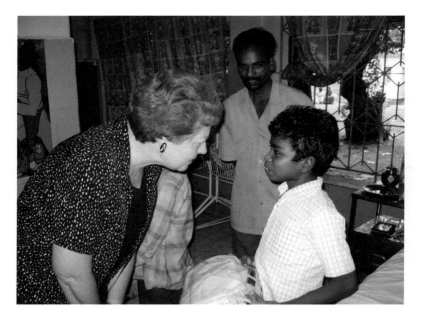

Have a conversation with a child not related to you. Ask questions. Listen.

Who are your heroes?
SHEROS Maya Angelou says, "We all need sheros and heroes." Think of a person you admire. Select one of their characteristics that you would HEROS like to emulate. Do it.

Create and maintain a group of close friends and relatives, referred to by some researchers as a "convoy," to go through life with you. Care for and sustain each other. Physician Rachel Naomi Remen says, "After all these years, I have begun to wonder if the secret of living well is not in having all the answers but in pursuing unanswerable questions in good company."

Love well, without being domineering or demanding. However, be prepared; as the artist called Sark warns us,

"Love is messy, inconvenient, and often annoying. This is not spoken of enough."

Chapter Three
LEARNING

"Live as if you were to die tomorrow. Learn as if you were to live forever." –Mahatma Gandhi

We who are older feel both exhilaration and vulnerability at trying to learn something new. That's because, beginning in middle age, age-related changes in our brains may lead to problems with memory, attention span, and mental focus. We're told that diet, exercise, and mental training can help to lessen the losses, and that we can learn to compensate for changing mental abilities. Let's see how we might train ourselves to use the remarkable brain power that we have.

Find a lifelong learning or adult education organization and take courses. Teach some. Follow your passions. For example, there are over 100 Osher Lifelong Learning Institutes on college and university campuses across the United States. They provide educational programs for people over fifty "who are interested in learning for the joy of learning."

Choose an author or composer you admire, but whose work you don't know very well. Examine that body of work. Decipher why you like it. What are the joys? gifts? liabilities? weaknesses?

Choose an author or composer whose work you are uncertain or negative about. Examine his or her work. What are the joys? gifts? liabilities? weaknesses? If you are still not interested, why not?

Do something really, really well. For example, learn to do tricks with a yo-yo or juggle. Practice. Try for excellence.

Develop a cooking specialty. It could be something simple, like salsa, bread or an unusual dessert. Share it with people who live nearby.

Study some aspect of the theater— dramaturgy, costumes, scenery, set design, playwriting. Support your local community theater groups. Volunteer.

ON STAGE

Try a new computer maneuver. You can ask a child to help you. Be sure your system is backed up before trying anything different. If you are uncomfortable with your computer, consider signing up for a class.

Take photographs with your cell phone. Yes, you can. Your grandchildren or neighbor children will show you. Send them to people by e-mail. Yes, they'll show you that, too. Or you can read the directions that came with your phone.

Read T.S. Eliot's *Four Quartets*. What does he suggest about how to live? Why does he say "Old men ought to be explorers"?

Read what young people are reading, like Harry Potter or the latest series books. Re-read, with your present wisdom, something you read as a teenager. Keep in mind P. J. O'Rourke's advice, "Always read stuff that will make you look good if you die in the middle of it."

Chapter Four

"I dream things that never were; and I say 'why not?'"
–George Bernard Shaw, *Back to Methuselah*

How can we use our competencies in new ways, or enhance the old ways? Where do we want to channel our skills, energies, and passions to make something new? What keeps us from trying? While we're not all artists or scientists, we are all capable of new self-expression—new perspectives, putting things together in a unique way. Psychiatrist Gene Cohen says, "Creativity is the ability to think about something in a new way," and finds that the right "combination of knowledge, experience, and emotional readiness occurs most dramatically in later life." Now is the time to seize the opportunity. We don't need to wait any longer to see what we can do.

If creativity was a part of your work life, continue it in some form. There are many, many examples of creative work in late life; for example, Frank Lloyd Wright designed the Guggenheim Museum in New York at age 91. Operatic tenor Hugues Cuenod made his Metropolitan Opera debut at 85. Scholars of the humanities have noted that some older artists, writers, and musicians go beyond their earlier work. What is called their "late style" is not serene and mellow, but more complex, more connected with future work in their field.

Perhaps creativity has been a secondary part of your life: now you can concentrate on it. After 60 years of painting for her own pleasure, Carmen Herrera sold her first artwork at age 89, and has become, to quote a *New York Times* headline, "the Hot New Thing in Painting."

If you have not developed your creative capacities, you now have time to explore and focus on them. You may feel vulnerable and awkward about trying. Go ahead anyway. Make some of what Dr. Lawrence-Lightfoot calls "unlikely choices." As the title of a book about innovation states,

Whoever Makes the Most Mistakes Wins.

Write a poem or song.

Make up a children's story, or rewrite a familiar one and change it. Teresa Celsi did that with *The Fourth Little Pig*.

Learn to draw cartoons.

Write a memoir piece
about an important
time in your life.
Send it to everyone.
Continue to write
about things and
people who
are no longer here.
Preserve the
experiences.

Make a piece of jewelry from wire you get at the hardware store. Wear it.

Go around taking photographs of something, like

doors, or red flowers, or stray dogs.

Show and discuss your collection.

Find a plant you've not previously tended. Grow it in a pot. Herbs, for instance, can fit on a windowsill. Or, if you have a garden, redesign a flower bed. Flowers, like people, can sometimes benefit from trimming or even transplanting. Perhaps you could create an area that attracts butterflies and hummingbirds.

Explore woodworking. Have you ever tried to whittle? Take a pottery class. Check with your community center to see what classes are offered. Invite a grandchild or friend to come with you.

Chapter Five

Helping

"…the deepest part of us wants us to give something back, to leave the campground a little better than we found it."

–Robert Raines,
   A Time to Live: Seven Tasks of Creative Aging

In late life, we may find that we take a broader view of the world and its problems, and can bring our experience to bear on thinking about solutions. We have visions of how things might be better, and we may be impatient with what is actually being done, or not done. We now have time to get involved. What might we do?

Adopt a cause. Speak up. Maggie Kuhn, founder of the Gray Panthers at age 65, said, "Speak your mind, even if your voice shakes…When you least expect it, someone may actually listen to what you have to say." Who is going to work for peace, take care of the environment, help other people? We are.

GRAY PANTHERS

Age and Youth in Action

Personally assist people in need. Work once a week in a soup kitchen or homeless shelter. Tutor a child who's having a difficult time. Or go to Kenya.

Start your own 501(c)3 charity. Donald E. Messer has been passionately concerned about persons infected and affected

by HIV/ AIDS for many years. Upon his retirement, he chose to devote himself to being a voice for many who are stigmatized and marginalized. He created The Center for the Church and Global AIDS which raises funds to provide support worldwide for programs of education, prevention, care and treatment.

What is your passion? How could you get involved?

Political activist Jerry Rubin says,

"Don't tell me what you believe. Show me what you do twenty-four hours a day, and I'll tell you what you believe."

Thank someone unexpectedly. For example, call UPS or FedEx or the U.S. Postal Service and thank them for delivering on time. If there's a specific service person involved, remember the name and be sure the message gets to their supervisor.

As you are financially able, tip extravagantly sometimes. Tip cab drivers, wait staff or other service providers 50%. With small expenditures, like a cup of coffee, tip 100%. Or more. Never mind whether you agree with the whole system of tipping; it

is in place, and people depend upon it.

Organize or join a public demonstration. A group of grandmothers stands on Fifth Avenue near Rockefeller Center, holding placards and handing out leaflets, in silent opposition to wars. They, and others who choose to join them, have been doing this every Wednesday since January 14, 2004.

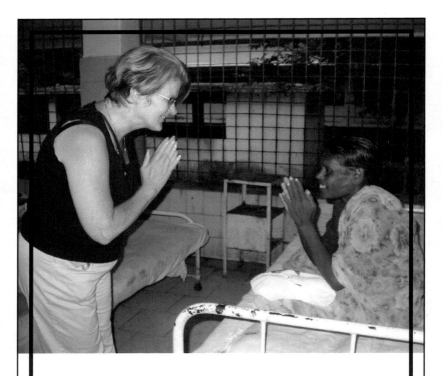

Do one small thing. The needs can be so great that we become overwhelmed. But one by one, we can make a difference. Helen Keller said,

> *"I long to accomplish*
> *a great and noble task,*
> *but it is my chief duty to*
> *accomplish small tasks as if*
> *they were great and noble."*

Listen to and encourage others in their endeavors toward a better world. Learn about The Elders, a group of eminent global leaders—such as Jimmy

Carter, Nelson Mandela, Desmond Tutu–who offer consultation, experience, and influence for promoting peace and human rights.

Is there something like that for you to do?

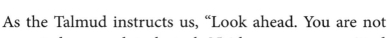

As the Talmud instructs us, "Look ahead. You are not expected to complete the task. Neither are you permitted to lay it down."

43

Chapter Six

Managing

"Surviving is important, but thriving is elegant."
–Maya Angelou

As we age, we must adapt to the altered circumstances of our life over which we have little or no control. We grieve for what is lost. And then we draw upon every aspect of our resilience and we move on. After a lifetime, we have our own particular coping skills. We use those, and develop new ones. You can deal with adversity because you've done it so many times before. Psychiatrist Dennis Charney, an expert on resilience, says the greatest surprise of his career is the hidden capacity of most people to deal with adversity. In other words, you're stronger than you realize.

You may develop a new and unwelcome health problem. You may ask, in the words of writer Dorothy Parker, "What fresh hell is this?" and swear a lot. After that, you'll figure out how to deal with it. Look for new ideas, devices, treatments, helpers, experts. Find or establish a network that will support you. The website www. whatfriendsdo.com has ideas about how to be a friend to someone who is struggling with a health problem.

Identify essential core actions. Make a list of small things to do everyday to tap into the deeper meaning and energy of your life.

Make and implement a plan of health and wellness for yourself. Include nutrition, exercise, and yoga. What would keep you from carrying this out?

Let go of some burdens. There may be responsibilities you no longer need to carry. Philosopher Lin Yutang said, "The wisdom of life consists in the elimination of nonessentials." Furthermore, the *Tao Te Ching*, an ancient Chinese wisdom text, tells us, "In the pursuit of knowledge, every day something is added. In the practice of the Tao, every day something is dropped."

Avoid phony positive thinking.
Be realistically irritable sometimes.
Life is hard.

Tell people what you need. Ask for rides.
Ask for help in lifting and carrying.

Pause for gratitude, for what you have and what you are, and for the people who are with you.

"Life is a gift. That's why they call it the present."
—UNKNOWN

Chapter Seven

Playing

"When you die,
God and the angels
will hold you accountable
for all the pleasures
you were allowed in life
that you denied yourself."
–Anonymous

Laugh, play, and enjoy. The later years of life can be a time of challenging old inhibitions, of finding deeper emotions, including humor and laughter. Life is often ridiculous. Join in the fun.

Buy a shirt that makes a statement or a political message. Wear it.

Age and treachery always win out over youth and skill!

Go to a toy store. Buy yourself a toy. Play with it. Don't give it to a child. Display it in your home.

Buy a clown nose.
Wear it to a children's party.
Don't explain.

Try playing a new musical instrument. It could be a penny whistle. A harmonica. Or a banjo. Or get out the guitar you haven't played since the 1960s and sign up for some lessons. Violinist Itzhak Perlman said, "Sometimes it is the artist's task to find out how much music you can still make with what you have left."

Dance, if you're able. If not with your legs, wave your arms. Toddlers do this—if they can't walk well, they dance with the rest of their bodies.

Sing loudly,
even if you can't sing.

Anthropologist Angeles Arrien suggests we ask ourselves "Where in my life did I stop singing? Where in my life did I stop dancing?" Sing walking down the street and while waiting in line. Hum tunes of unknown origin. Sing along with piped-in music played in stores, waiting rooms, and elevators. Nietzsche noted, "Without music, life would be a mistake."

Give yourself treats. Novelist Iris Murdock says, "One of the secrets of a happy life is continuous small treats."

Epilogue

"Choose joy. Cultivate it. Squeeze life … When you die, you want someone to cancel all your appointments."
  –The Rev. Dr. Thad Lee McGhee

"Find some particular thing your soul craves for nourishment and do it."
  –Audre Lord

"Here you are, alive. Would you like to make a comment?"
  –Mary Oliver

"If you ask me what I have come into this world to do, I will tell you: I have come to live out loud."
  –Emile Zola

"The game is scheduled, we have to play it—we might as well win."
  –Phoenix Suns' locker room

"Since this precious human life can be used in powerfully beneficial or destructive ways, and is itself most fragile, make good use of it now."
    –His Holiness the Dalai Lama

"So let us be about the task; it is for today, and for times we shall never see. The materials are very precious, and they are very perishable. Amen."
    –Benediction, Minneapolis church

Show us how precious each day is; teach us to be fully here.
    –Psalm 90:12

References

Arrien, Angeles. *The Four-fold Way: Walking the Paths of the Warrior, Teacher, Healer and Visionary*. New York: HarperCollins, 1993.

Angelou, Maya. www.goodreads.com/author/quotes/3503.Maya_Angelou

Baker, Dan, & Stauth, Cameron. *What Happy People Know: How the New Science of Happiness Can Change Your Life for the Better*. Emmaus, PA: Rodale, 2002.

Bridges, William. *Transitions: Making Sense of Life's Changes* (2nd Ed.). Cambridge, MA: DaCapo Press, 2004.

Celsi, Teresa. *The Fourth Little Pig*. Milwaukee: Raintree Publishers, 1990.

Chodron, Pema. The power of patience: Antidote to escalation. In McLeod, Melvin (Ed.). *Mindful Politics: A Buddhist Guide to Making the World a Better Place*. Boston: Wisdom Publications, 2006. P. 141-146.

Cohen, Gene. *The Creative Age: Awakening Human Potential in the Second Half of Life*. New York: Avon Books, 2000.

Eliot, George. www.goodreads.com/author/quotes/173.George_Eliot

Eliot, T.S. *Four Quartets*. New York: Harcourt, Brace and Co., 1943.

Farson, Richard, & Keyes, Ralph. *Whoever Makes the Most Mistakes Wins: The Paradox of Innovation*. New York: The Free Press, 2002.

Haberman, Clyde. "On 5th Ave., a Grandmothers' Protest as Endless as the Wars." *New York Times*, 5/7/10, A18.

Kornfield, Jack. T*he Art of Forgiveness, Lovingkindness, and Peace*. New York: Bantam Books, 2002.

Kuhn, Maggie, with Long, Christina, & Quinn, Laura. *No Stone Unturned: The Life and Times of Maggie Kuhn*. New York: Ballantine Books, 1991.

Lawrence-Lightfoot, Sarah. *The Third Chapter: Passion, Risk, and Adventure in the 25 Years After 50*. New York: Farrar, Straus & Giroux, 2009.

McGehee, The Reverend Dr. Thad Lee. Lecture, "Laughter in Living," Bay View, MI, August 31, 2009.

Nietzsche, Friedrich. *Twilight of the Idols*. New York: Oxford Univ. Press, 1888/1998.

Oliver, Mary. "The Summer Day," in *House of Light*. Boston: Beacon Press, 1990.

_____*Long Life: Essays and Other Writing*. Cambridge, MA: DaCapo Press, 2004.

Parker, Dorothy. *The Portable Dorothy Parker*. New York: Viking Press, 1973.

Perlman, Itzhak. Cited in Dossey, Larry. *The Extraordinary Healing Power of Ordinary Things: Fourteen Natural Steps to Health and Happiness*. New York: Harmony Books, 2006. P. 114.

Raines, Robert. *A Time to Live: Seven Tasks of Creative Aging*. New York: Dutton, 1997.

Remen, Rachel Naomi. *My Grandfather's Blessings: Stories of Strength, Refuge, and Belonging*. New York: Riverhead Books, Penguin Putnam, Inc., 2000.

Rowe, John W. & Kahn, Robert L. *Successful Aging*. New York: Dell, 1998.

Sark. *The Bodacious Book of Succulence*. New York: Fireside/ Simon & Schuster, 1998.

_____*Transformation Soup*. New York: Fireside, Simon & Schuster, 2000.

Shaw, George Bernard. *Back to Methuselah: A Metabiological Pentateuch*. New York: Brentano's, 1921.

Sontag, Deborah. "At 94, She's the Hot New Thing in Painting, and Enjoying It."(Carmen Herrera). *New York Times*, 12/20/09, 1, 29.

Southwick, Steven M., Litz, Brett T., Charney, Dennis, and Friedman, Matthew J. *Resilience and Mental Health: Challenges Across the Lifespan*. Cambridge, UK: Cambridge University Press, 2011.

Vaillant, George E. *Aging Well: Surprising Guideposts to a Happier Life from the Landmark Harvard Study of Adult Development*. Boston: Little, Brown & Co, 2002.

About the Authors

Bonnie J. Messer, Ph.D., licensed psychologist in private practice in Colorado, counsels adults of all ages. Her specialties include coping with transitions, grief and loss, stress management, self esteem, and couples communication. She has taught university courses in Human Development and Social Work. Publications include *Dealing with Change* (Abingdon Press) and "Loving, Honoring, and Cherishing" with Donald E. Messer in *Reflections on Marriage and Spiritual Growth*, Andrew J. Weaver and Carolyn Stapleton, editors (Abingdon Press). Bonnie may be contacted at bjmesser@comcast.net.

Marjorie A. Bayes, Ph.D., a retired clinical psychologist, has held faculty positions in the Yale University School of Medicine Department of Psychiatry and Smith College School for Social Work. She established independent practices of psychotherapy in Northampton, MA, and Denver, CO. She has taught courses in Human Development, worked on community projects for senior citizens, and presented workshops on "Growing Old: Attitudes, Fears, and Life Development." Author of several academic journal articles, she also co-edited an anthology, *Women and Mental Health* (Basic Books/ HarperCollins). She is a member of the Gray Panthers. Marjorie may be contacted at bayeswashburn@mac.com.

Susan Bell is an illustrator, graphic designer and digital artist in Centennial, Colorado. She returned to school at the age of 52 to learn digital design and imaging. She works in a variety of mediums both in her Communication Design work at St. Andrew United Methodist Church and freelance work. Susan is thrilled to be illustrating this book with Bonnie and Marjorie. Contact her at susan.bell.design@gmail.com.

Made in the USA
Charleston, SC
27 October 2012